SPIRITUAL TRAVAIL

Stephen Kaung

Available from:

Christian Testimony Ministry
4424 Huguenot Road
Richmond, Virginia 23235

www.christiantestimonyministry.com

PRINTED IN USA

CONTENTS

Stephen Kaung spoke the messages contained in this booklet at the Northeast Christian Weekend Conference, Long Beach Island, New Jersey in October 2009. The spoken words have been transcribed by permission with only minimal editing for clarity. Unless otherwise indicated, Scripture quotations are from the *New Translation* by J. N. Darby.

Chapter 1

WHAT IS SPIRITUAL TRAVAIL?

Galatians 4:19—My children, of whom I again travail in birth until Christ shall have been formed in you.

Isaiah 53:11—He [Jesus] shall see of the fruit of the travail of his soul, and shall be satisfied: by his knowledge shall my righteous servant instruct many in righteousness; and he shall bear their iniquities.

John 16:21—A woman, when she gives birth to a child, has grief because her hour has come; but when the child is born, she no longer remembers the trouble, on account of the joy that a man has been born into the world.

Dear Lord, we praise and thank Thee for gathering us together. It is truly the prayer of our hearts that there is nothing between us and Thee. We praise and thank Thee that Thou has accomplished a full salvation and there is no reason why there should be any distance. So Lord, we just cast ourselves upon Thee, believing that Thou does remove every distance between us and Thee. Thou has drawn us into Thy very presence that when we see Thy glory, we may hear Thy voice, and by Thy Spirit we may be transformed and conformed to the image of Thy beloved Son. Dear Lord, we do confess that this theme is beyond us, but we praise and thank Thee knowing that Thou who art faithful has called us, and Thou will perform and perfect that which Thou has begun in us. And with this we commit ourselves to Thee for this time. May Thy name be glorified. We pray in the name of our Lord Jesus. Amen.

I have to confess that when I first heard the theme of this conference was "Spiritual Travail" I was frightened because immediately Moses arose in my mind. He pleaded before God for the children of Israel and was willing even to have his name blotted out from the book of life for the sake of the people.

Then I thought of the apostle Paul and how he travailed before God. He travailed for his own kinsmen and was willing even to have his name blotted out from the book of life for his brethren's sake.

People like Elijah and Daniel also rose in my mind. I thought of Praying Hyde of India and how he prayed before God. I thought also of Rees Howells of South Wales, the intercessor. So when these pictures arose in my mind, I trembled. Who am I to talk about spiritual travail? How much do we really know what spiritual travail is? And more than that, how much are we involved in that spiritual travail? Is it too high for us? Is it too deep for us? Is it something beyond us that we should not talk about? Then the Lord comforted me. He told me that I am the fruit of the travail of His soul. And not only am I the fruit of His travail but I can recall people who travailed in prayer before God for me, and here I am.

There was a famous person in history by the name of Saint Augustine. He was a brilliant young man, and he was a professor of rhetoric in the university. At that time a professor of rhetoric was the highest rank in the university, but he lived a very dissipated life. But thank God, he had a mother—Monica. It was the prayers and the tears of his mother that brought him to the Savior.

We are all the fruit of the travail of the soul of our Lord Jesus. If He had not travailed for us where would we be? And probably we can also recall the story of how we came to the Lord. Maybe our parents, maybe a friend, maybe someone who knew us pleaded before God for us, and today we are the fruit of the travail of their soul.

IS SPIRITUAL TRAVAIL NECESSARY?

As I was thinking of these things it really encouraged me. So I thought: why spiritual travail? Is it that important? Is it necessary? Is it absolutely needed in every one of us? Or is it just for a few select ones like Rees Howells, Praying Hyde, Paul, Moses? Is this the exclusive right or favor that God has given to them? And who are we even to talk about spiritual travail, not to say to really engage in spiritual travail? Is it something just for a select few? Or is it for us common brothers and sisters? Is every one of us to be engaged in spiritual travail, and why? It is the will of God. It is because of the One who travailed for our salvation. He has put His life in us, and that life has the element of travail in us. He has put His Spirit in us, and His Spirit pleads within our spirit, helping us in this matter of spiritual travail. So let us remember that this spiritual travail is not for someone who has reached a certain spiritual stature and then they will be engaged in spiritual travail. We may be just a babe in Christ, just saved, but we too should begin to learn this lesson of spiritual travail. It should be the mark of every believer because it is God's will. God wants each and every one of us whom He has justified to be glorified. He wants each and every one of us not only saved but to be conformed to the image of His beloved Son.

But we ask the question: How? He has begun a good work in us, but how is He going to complete it? And in completing it is there anything that He requires or demands of us that we should be engaged in? As I thought of these things I began to realize that spiritual travail is a calling to every believer, from the littlest one to the greatest one. Do not be intimidated by a few brothers and sisters who have reached such a height in their experience in spiritual travail that you do not even begin to travail in your spirit. So with that I am encouraged, and I do hope that every one of us will be encouraged.

When you are listening to this message of spiritual travail, do not ever say, "This is not for me; this is only for those who have reached a certain spiritual stature." Yes, the more you grow in the Lord the deeper spiritual travail will be your experience. But if you do not begin from the very beginning, you will not reach it. So I am encouraged for all brothers and sisters—especially the young people—that you will open your heart believing that the One who travailed for you on Calvary's cross lives in you, and His life is a life of travail. And we need to allow that life to really grow in each and every one of us.

I am thinking especially of the imminent return of our Lord Jesus. Why is it we have waited for twenty centuries for His return? We are now in the beginning of the twenty-first century; why the delay? The fault, the reason does not lie with our Lord Jesus. Every bridegroom is anxious to receive his bride. It is the bride who is not prepared. Can it be that the reason why the church, the bride of our Lord Jesus has not been ready for Him for these twenty centuries is the lack of spiritual travail? God's people have received the grace of God, and yet we do not allow that grace to work in our lives and make us gracious that we may be able to hasten the return of the Lord. The responsibility is upon us, and I am afraid the reason for it is the lack of spiritual travail. Because we do not have that spiritual travail, we do not grow spiritually. Because we do not have that spiritual travail, people are not saved. Because we do not have spiritual travail, the body is not completed. Is it because of the lack of spiritual travail? So I do hope that every brother and sister will really see the importance, the urgency. God is pleading for us to be engaged in His heart's travail so that His perfect will can be completed.

SPIRITUAL TRAVAIL BRINGS BIRTH

What is spiritual travail? How can we be engaged in this spiritual travail? In the dictionary the word *travail* means "a physical or mental exertion, effort, trial." It is usually accompanied by tribulation, anguish, agony, and it also describes child birth. In the Greek original you will find the same thought. It is travail, an exercise within our spirit. It is tribulation, suffering, and agony, but thank God it results in birth. Now if it is travail without giving birth that is a terrible thing. But when you think of travail leading to birth, isn't that promising?

I remember when our Lord Jesus was with His disciples before His crucifixion. After He had instituted the Lord's Table, He said, "This is My body for you; this do in remembrance of Me." And He took the cup and blessed it and said, "This is the blood that sealed that covenant, the new covenant. Remember this." And after the Lord's Supper He conversed with His disciples. The disciples were sorrowful because they sensed something was going to happen. They sensed that the Lord Jesus was leaving them. They had left everything to follow the Lord and now the Lord was going to leave them. So our Lord Jesus tried to comfort them and said, "Do not be grieved. I will leave you but I will come again." Then He said, "You will be grieved, and the world will be happy. But just like a woman when she is in travail, there is pain and grief for a time, but after a child is born all these will be forgotten, and she will rejoice because a child is born into this world" (see John 16:21).

So when we think of spiritual travail, it is something very positive. It is something that will bring us into birth. Then I began to think of what our Lord Jesus said, "In the world you have tribulation but be of good cheer, I have overcome the world." Every one who is born into this world will go through tribulation. The wisest of men, Solomon, wrote a book called Ecclesiastes. He became a preacher, and what is the message that he preached? Out of his great wisdom and through all his manifold experiences he told us that he tried everything under the sun, and then he wrote this book of Ecclesiastes. It describes the world and worldly travail. Everybody is in travail, not only Christians but non Christians; the world itself is in travail.

THE WORLD TRAVAILS

In Ecclesiastes 1:1, 8, 11, 18 it says, "The words of the Preacher, the son of David, king in Jerusalem. Vanity of vanities, saith the Preacher, vanity of vanities! All is vanity...All things are full of toil; none can express it. The eye is not satisfied with seeing, nor the ear filled with hearing...There is no remembrance of former things; neither shall there be remembrance of things that are to come with those who shall live afterwards...For in much wisdom is much vexation, and he that increaseth knowledge increaseth sorrow."

In Ecclesiastes 2:11, 22-23 it says, "Then I looked on all the works that my hands had wrought, and on the labour that it had cost me to do them; and behold, all was vanity and pursuit of the wind, and there was no profit under the sun...For what will man have of all his labour and of the striving of his heart, wherewith he hath wearied himself under the sun? For all his days are sorrows, and his travail vexation: even in the night his heart taketh no rest. This also is vanity."

The whole book describes what worldly travail is. Everybody is travailing. Everybody is exercising. Everybody is in pain, but what is the result? If you travail for the world it does not give birth. On the contrary, it produces death. Now that is worldly travail. Are you in that category? We should not be. Thank God He has removed us out of this world and put us in the kingdom of the Son of His love. So our travail is a different kind of travail. It is called spiritual travail, and this spiritual travail results in birth. So that is why every believer should be involved in this spiritual travail.

WHY THE PAIN FOR BIRTH?

Brothers and sisters, we are the fruit of the travail of God. But I often wonder, is it necessary that with travail for birth there has to be pain, suffering, anguish, agony? God is love, and because He loves us He travails. But in the very beginning when He created the heavens and the earth, did it cause God suffering, pain, tribulation? God put Adam to sleep and took something out of his side to build a woman. We often say that is the first operation in the world, but it was a painless operation because God put Adam to sleep. There was no pain involved. So where does that pain that always accompanies travail come from? You remember when Adam and Eve sinned against God, He came into the garden and pronounced His judgment. In Genesis 3:16 God's judgment upon the woman was that He would increase her travail in childbirth, and in pain she would bring forth children. So I wonder if that is where these two things are related, that there must be pain in travail for birth. Is it because there is sin in this world? And when sin comes in, the scene is totally different. It becomes a universal law that wherever there is travail there is pain. Put it in another way: where there is no suffering there is no birth. This has become a universal law. This is the reason why travail is always accompanied with suffering.

Consider how our God has travailed for us for our salvation. We are so familiar with John 3:16: "God so loved the world that He gave His only begotten Son that whosoever believeth in Him shall not perish but have everlasting life." Everything begins with the love of God. If there is no love there is no suffering. "God so loved the world" and the world here especially refers to the people in this world. God so loved the people He created that He gave His only begotten Son.

God has only one begotten Son. They were together from the very beginning. They were not only equal but

They were one. They had never left each other. They loved each other; They understood each other. In everything They were in perfect harmony. And this love between Them was increasing. And it is out of that love for His beloved Son that He created the universe, especially man. Man is a special creation of God because there is nothing else created after His image according to His likeness. Everything is created by God but it is created by His wisdom, by His power. Only man in the whole universe is created in His own image after His own likeness. Why? It is because He wants to give man to be His Son's life companion, and in order to be His Son's life companion he has to be like His Son. Otherwise they do not fit. So it is out of love that God created man. But unfortunately, human beings, who received the greatest gift of God in creation, rebelled against Him. And because of this we were separated from God, even turning ourselves against God as His enemies. How we sinned against Him! The Bible tells us that all have sinned and come short of the glory of God.

What is the glory of God? The glory of God is Himself. We come short of His glory because we are not like Him. We are the very opposite of what He is, and that hurts Him more than anything else. Sometimes when we are preaching the gospel to unbelievers, we mention Romans 1, listing all the terrible sins that man has committed in order to convince these people that they are sinful. But the Bible says, "…for sin because they do not believe in Me." That is the greatest sin in the world. If you do not believe in the Lord Jesus that is the greatest sin in the world because this is the greatest gift God has given to man. Everything is involved there, and if you resist Him you resist His love. But thank God, He does not forsake us. We who have sinned should be left behind, judged forever, but it is God's love that He gave us His only begotten Son. Think on that.

ABRAHAM GAVE UP HIS SON

When we talk about this, we always think about Abraham. When Abraham was a hundred years old, he got a son. Now when you are thirty years old and get a son, how happy you are! But when Abraham was a hundred years old and got a son, he was the treasure of his heart— Isaac. That gladdened his heart; it made him laugh. And then God said, "Take your son, your only begotten son." Now God makes it very difficult. "Go three days journey (He gave him plenty of time to think.) and offer him to Me." If we did not know God we would think God is so hard, but Abraham knew God. He got up early in the morning, took his son, prepared everything for the sacrifice, and went to Mt. Moriah. He was going to sacrifice his son because he loved God more than anything else, and he believed that God would bring Isaac into life.

GOD TRAVAILED IN THE GIVING OF HIS SON

When you read this story, how do you feel? But if you can multiply it millions and billions of times, think how God felt when He gave His only begotten Son to us. His love is billions and billions of times deeper than any human parent, and in His travail for our souls He was willing to give His beloved Son who is incomparable with any human son or daughter. What a sacrifice! What suffering it must be to God!

Throughout the life of our Lord Jesus on earth, again and again and again, the heavens opened and a voice came from heaven: "This is My beloved Son in whom I have found My delight." You can see how much God loved His beloved Son, and yet when you read Isaiah 53:10 it says, "God crushed Him on Calvary's cross." Is it an easy thing to do? The Son had pleased Him throughout His life, even throughout eternity, and the Father crushed Him.

When our Lord Jesus was crucified, from nine o'clock to twelve o'clock it was man who crucified Him. Man mocked Him, and Satan surrounded Him. But during those three hours our Lord Jesus never said a word about Himself. The Father was with Him. He could pray, "Forgive them for they know not what they do." But then the scene suddenly changed. Matthew 27 tells us that from twelve o'clock until three o'clock the sun hid its face. There was darkness all around, and it was during that period our Lord cried out: "My God, my God, why has Thou forsaken Me?" The Father turned His face away so He could not see the suffering of His beloved Son. What love! What sacrifice! What agony! What birth pain! And remember, we are the fruit of the travail of God the Father's heart.

JESUS TRAVAILED AS THE LAMB OF GOD

Then you think of our Lord Jesus Himself. He was before His Father as His nursling. He rejoiced before His Father creating all things according to the will of His Father. And yet the Bible tells us, even before the foundation of the world, He was the Lamb of God (see I Peter 1). In other words, before God created anything, our Lord Jesus, the beloved Son of God, had already offered Himself to be the Lamb of God because God knew everything. God knew what would happen. After the world was created and man was created, what would happen to man? What would happen to this world? God saw it all. May I use human words? God hesitated a little bit and the Son stepped in and said, "Father, go ahead. If this is what You want to do, do it. I am willing to offer Myself to be the Lamb of God." Our Lord Jesus is the Lamb of God before He came into this world.

John the Baptist looked at Him and said, "Behold, the Lamb of God who takes away the sin of the world." But even before He came into this world, in eternity past, before time began, before the world was created, He had already offered Himself to be the Lamb. Therefore the Bible tells us He was the Lamb slain from the foundation of the world. It was upon the basis of Him offering Himself to the Father to be the Lamb that God began to create the universe. And when the universe began, our Lord Jesus, as the Lamb of God, was slain from the beginning of the world. Can you imagine the love behind it? Can you imagine the travail, the suffering, the pain, the anguish, the sorrow, and yet in the fullness of time our Lord Jesus came, born of woman, born under law, that He may deliver us from the curse of the Law and receive sonship. "The Word became flesh and tabernacled among men, full of grace and truth" (John 1:14). Throughout the life of our Lord Jesus He pleased the Father! He said nothing out of Himself. He did nothing out of Himself. He was always under the timing of the Father's will. His face was towards Jerusalem. He came, He was born, not to live but to die.

We all remember the scene of Gethsemane. Our Lord Jesus was a perfect Man. By perfect it means that on the one hand He was sinless. He had never known what sin is. He had never committed any sin, so He could not even know what sin is. But being a perfect Man His feeling, His senses, His will, His soul-life must be hundreds, thousands, billions times sharper than ours. How must He feel when He was to become sin for us? The sin of the whole world was heaped upon Him. The Bible says, "He was made sin for us." He not only bore our sins but He was made sin for us. In the sight of God He was sin itself. How terrible that is! No wonder our Lord could not stand it and He prayed, "Father, if it is possible let this cup pass from Me, but I have come for this hour. Glorify Your name."

In the garden of Gethsemane the Bible tells us how He was oppressed in His spirit, how He was grieved in His soul. He prayed until His sweat came out as drops of blood in agony. "Father, if it is possible let this cup pass from Me but not My will, Thy will be done." And when Judas came with the crowds to take the Lord, our Lord said, "Must I not drink the cup that the Father has given Me?" He went to the cross, and from twelve o'clock to three o'clock was the time He was made sin for us. And God, who is the righteous One, the Judge of the world, crushed Him, putting Him to death. He sentenced Him to death in order to put sin away for us.

What agony! What travail our Lord Jesus has gone through! And it is for you and for me. We are the fruit of the travail of His soul.

THE HOLY SPIRIT TRAVAILS TO BRING BIRTH

Think of the Holy Spirit, the third Person in the Godhead. How the Holy Spirit travailed! When we think about when we were saved and what God has done for us, probably our first thought will be: "Thank God, my sins are rolled away. I am forgiven. I am justified. Now I have peace in my conscience. Now I can face God. Now one day I will go to heaven." But these are the least of the grace of God in His salvation. Yes, thank God, when I am saved, not only my sins are forgiven but He has given me His own life. Now the life of God, the life of Christ is my life. He is here in me. Thank God for this life. And thank God, when He gave this life of Christ to us, at the same time the Holy Spirit came and dwelt in our new spirit. The Holy Spirit came as a Guardian of that new life, as the One who is responsible to bring that life into maturity, to see to it that we will be transformed and be like Christ. Anything that is not like Christ He will judge. He will touch our conscience, make us uncomfortable until we are willing to repent and return to Him. He is doing this great job day by day, hour by hour, minute by minute because He will never leave us nor forsake us. He is always in us for only one reason and that is to see that the new life, the eternal life, the life of Christ in us will be given all the needed help to be brought into maturity, that we may be transformed and conformed to the image of God's beloved Son, that He might be the firstborn among many brethren. This is why the Holy Spirit is in us. And He said that the Holy Spirit will never leave us nor forsake us.

When our Lord Jesus was in the flesh, He had to leave us to return to the Father, but the another Comforter of His like came to dwell in us forever. Do you think that the Holy Spirit in you is free from travailing, from pain, from suffering, from anguish? Since you are born again, since you have received the Holy Spirit, how much have you cooperated with the Holy Spirit? How much have you listened to the still small voice? How much are you walking in the light of life? How much have you obeyed Him? The Bible says, "Grieve not the Holy Spirit" (see Ephesians 4:30).

How much we must have grieved Him! If we try to add up all the grief that we have piled upon Him, what will happen? Humanly speaking He will die; but He never died. Even though we grieve Him, He will not leave us nor forsake us. How we grieve Him beyond measure! We grieve Him because we want to have our own way. We want to live our own life. We will not allow the life of Christ to grow in us. Our self-life wants to grow.

"Quench not the Holy Spirit" (I Thessalonians 5:19). How much we have quenched Him! We will not listen to Him. Do you know that when we are doing that, not only will the Holy Spirit suffer in pain to bring forth but we are the ones who suffer the loss. Think of that! No matter how we grieve Him, no matter how we quench Him, no matter how we disobey Him, He will not leave. He is still here in me, in you, continuing in His travailing pain in order to bring forth birth. Think of that!

When we think of all the travail, all the suffering that we have caused our Father, our Lord Jesus, the Holy Spirit, will not that bring us to shame? As the fruit of the travail of

His soul, what shall we do? On the one hand, is it not the right thing for us to do that we really appreciate all His travailing for us, giving ourselves totally to Him that love may complete His work. On the other hand, is it not that we should try to cooperate with Him in travailing, that is to say whatever He travails for we travail with Him. And that is the reason why I feel this matter of spiritual travail is our portion. Every one of us must be involved. And may the Lord show us how we can be involved in spiritual travail and what it will mean to God and His purpose.

Shall we pray:

Dear Lord, we do sense that we are standing on holy ground. Lord, reveal Thy travail to each and every one of us. Let Thy travail give us strength to respond not only to obey but to follow. Oh Lord, may the Spirit of Thy travail fall upon us that we may become a people that will travail with Thee for Thy eternal purpose to be fulfilled. We are here offering ourselves to Thee for Thou has called us. We cannot do it but Thou are able to perfect it. We ask in Thy precious name. Amen.

Chapter 2

THE FOUR-FOLD AREAS OF SPIRITUAL TRAVAIL

Philippians 3:8—But surely I count also all things to be loss on account of the excellency of the knowledge of Christ Jesus my Lord, on account of whom I have suffered the loss of all, and count them to be filth, that I may gain Christ.

Romans 8:18-27—For I reckon that the sufferings of this present time are not worthy to be compared with the coming glory to be revealed to us. For the anxious looking out of the creature expects the revelation of the sons of God: for the creature has been made subject to vanity, not of its will, but by reason of him who has subjected the same, in hope that the creature itself also shall be set free from the bondage of corruption into the liberty of the glory of the children of God. For we know that the whole creation groans together and travails in pain together until now. And not only that, but even we ourselves, who have the first-fruits of the Spirit, we also ourselves groan in ourselves, awaiting sonship, that is the redemption of our body. For we have been saved in hope; but hope seen is not hope; for what any one sees, why does he also hope? But if what we see not we hope, we expect in patience. And in like manner the Spirit joins also its help to our weakness; for we do not know what we should pray for as is fitting, but the Spirit itself makes intercession with groanings which cannot be uttered. But he who searches the hearts knows what is the mind of the Spirit, because he intercedes for saints according to God.

Colossians 1:24-29—Now, I rejoice in sufferings for you, and I fill up that which is behind of the tribulations of Christ in my flesh, for his body, which is the assembly [the church]; of which I became minister, according to the dispensation of God which is given me towards you to complete the word of God, the mystery which has been hidden from ages and from generations, but has now been made manifest to his saints; to whom God would make known what are the riches of the glory of this mystery among the nations, which is Christ in you the hope of glory: whom we announce, admonishing every man, and teaching every man, in all wisdom, to the end that we may present every man perfect in Christ. Whereunto also I toil, combating according to his working, which works in me in power.

Dear Lord, we want to praise and thank Thee for giving us the privilege of being at Thy table, Thy table of love, a love that loves to the very uttermost. Lord, may Thy love constrain each and every one of us, knowing that we are no longer ours but we are Yours. Give us that strong passion to gain Christ. Enable us to toil and labor, not for ourselves but for the completion of Thy eternal purpose. Oh dear Lord, we are here redeemed, not for ourselves but we are here for Thee, and may all that which Thou has purposed in Thy heart for us be fulfilled that God may be glorified. We commit this time into Thy hand, Lord. Speak, Thy servants heareth. We ask in Thy precious name. Amen.

As we fellowship on this matter of spiritual travail, at first look you may think it is a very heavy subject but the more you think about it, the more you see that it is grace. Grace begins the work and grace continues until the work is done. So when we are fellowshiping on spiritual travail, we are not to look at ourselves. Look to Him, the One who has travailed for us and brought us to this whole realm of travailing. From the very beginning to the very end it is grace, but it is grace received and grace responded to. We have received His grace and have been saved, and He has put His life in us. He has put His Spirit in us in order that by all His provision we may really come to know Him and know what is in His heart. If there is anything that can satisfy God's heart, we have to acknowledge it is not in ourselves; it is in Christ and Christ in us.

SPIRITUAL TRAVAIL BRINGS BIRTH UNTO SONSHIP

Spiritual travail is based upon the travailing of God for us. If He had not travailed for us we would not be here. We would have no means to travail in any way. We are called today to travail. It is our calling, but this calling is based upon what He has done for us. We thank God that we are the fruit of the travail of our Lord Jesus, and out of that travail He put His life in us. He gave His Holy Spirit to dwell in us without leaving us. Now what is the purpose behind it?

We say that travail is unto birth. But when there is birth, is that the final end? When a woman is in travail and gives birth to a child, she forgets all her anguish, tribulation, sorrow, and she is glad because a man has been born into this world. What comes out is a baby but what she expects is a man. Isn't it true that whenever there is any birth on this earth, even though that birth is beautiful, if that birth does not end in being a man or woman the joy will soon be turned into sorrow?

It is the same thing with God. It is out of the travail of our Lord Jesus on Calvary's cross that we are born into the family of God. Thank God for that. But what is the purpose behind it? Is it that God wants to have a kindergarten full of babies forever and ever? Not so! What God has in mind is His beloved Son. He wants to have many brethren for His Son. He wants His Son to be the firstborn among many brethren. The Son is the model, and He wants those who are born again to be transformed, to grow until we take upon ourselves the very image of His Son. We are to be characterized not only by His life but by the full expression of that life, to be Christ-like in order that we may be fit to be His eternal companion. Otherwise, God's purpose cannot be reached. That is the reason our Lord Jesus travailed for us, and that is the reason He calls us who are the fruit of His travail to travail with Him in our spirit that we, too, may fulfill all that God has ordained for us.

SPIRITUAL TRAVAIL IS A PRIVILEGE

This whole matter of spiritual travail is a *must*. If you look at it from God's view point, it is a must because this is God's eternal purpose. He wants His Son to be all and in all. He wants all of us who are babes in Christ to grow up to sonship. He wants to have a church, His own body, fully grown, fit to be the eternal bride of His beloved Son. And God has all this in His mind even before the foundation of the world. And thank God, He who has purposed it will fulfill it, and He has involved us in it. So this whole matter of spiritual travail is a privilege. It is a calling to every brother and sister, every born again child of God.

Now it is true that there are different levels of spiritual travail, and yet everybody is involved in it. As we grow in spiritual stature, that is as we grow in Christ Jesus, as we allow the life of Christ Jesus to take over more and more, then this spiritual travail will be fuller and fuller until God's purpose is done. So I hope that every brother and sister will be encouraged and know that this is a calling for every one of us.

SPIRITUAL TRAVAIL IS SUFFERING

We did ask this question. Is suffering necessary in travail? Briefly speaking, we may say travail is exertion, is exercise, but it is because there is sin in this world. Therefore it becomes a universal law that wherever there is travail, there is suffering. But thank God, that suffering is not negative at all. That suffering is positive because it brings us into the full fulfillment of God's purpose.

Let's look at travail from the physical standpoint. When we are born, we are a baby. We have life, but that is the beginning. We are born for the purpose of growing up into manhood and womanhood. As we are growing up, there are growing pains. Actually, every moment we are living in this world we are fighting a battle. It is a battle of life and death. We are born, and we have life, but all around us is death because sin is in this world. All the germs are around us. Every day we are living is a real battle. You have to fight against the death around you in order to grow. And this is why there are growing pains; otherwise, I would think we could grow without any pain. And this is why as we grow we have to exercise; we have to exert ourselves. We have to force ourselves, as it were, to overcome the death around us. Death is trying to intrude upon us to cut short that life. But thank God, He enables us to fight against it, and we will live and grow and mature into manhood and womanhood. Now this is physically speaking.

The same principle applies spiritually. Thank God we have been given a spiritual life. It is the life of Christ in us and this life is supposed to live. But as this life is living in this world it is surrounded by death and all kinds of spiritual germs. And when a believer, a Christian lives under that kind of situation in this present sinful world, there is opposition all around you, but the greatest opposition is within you.

Martin Luther said, "I am not afraid of the popes, the cardinals, the archbishops, the bishops, all that system, but I am afraid of the pope within me." That is our old life. That is our adamic life. That is the life that we received from our forefathers when we were born into this world. Unfortunately, this life is still with us; it resides in our soul. It seems to be still in control as it was for a long time. It is in control of our feelings; it is in control of our thoughts; it is in control even of our opinions and will. And even after we have received a new life, the life of Christ in our new spirit, unfortunately, in our soul this old adamic self *I* is still in charge. That is the reason for spiritual travail. Otherwise, as soon as we are saved, as soon as we receive the life within us, we would grow day and night quickly and arrive at maturity in no time. There would be no opposition. There would be no fighting, no travailing as it were. It would be supernaturally natural.

But why is it after we have believed in the Lord Jesus we do not have a smooth sailing to heaven? I am afraid among God's people we have a false sense of grace. We say it is all of grace; thank God for that. It is, and grace upon grace. No doubt about that, but our concept of grace is so cheap. We feel that because grace is free, therefore we can abuse it. Even when we abuse it, grace is still there. It is okay; we do not need the cross. We do not need to deny ourselves. We do not need to do anything. As soon as we are saved we will be taken on a sedan chair to heaven. That is a false concept. Worse than that, there is the prosperity gospel. Before we are saved we can be very poor, but now that we are saved we are a child of God, everything belongs to us.

I remember in the early sixties there was the so-called Child of God movement, those who said we are children of God. So they would go to the store and just take things because they said it all belonged to their Father.

That is a false concept of grace. True, everything is grace, but do not think that you are being carried on a sedan chair to heaven. When grace really works in our lives, it will produce a similar character within us. It will make us as loving, as gracious as the loving God and the gracious Lord, and because of that there will be travail. It is a spiritual travail.

THE FOUR AREAS OF SPIRITUAL TRAVAIL

Travail After Christ

The first area of spiritual travail is a travail after Christ. You remember the apostle Paul said in Philippians 3: "I count all things as dross for the excellency of the knowledge of Jesus Christ. I am willing to lose all things in order to gain Christ." Now do not confuse this. Is it not Christ who gains us? So why is it that the apostle Paul says, "gain Christ"? Has he not already been gained by Christ? On the road to Damascus the Lord met him, and the Lord gained him. Yet the apostle Paul said, "For the excellency of the knowledge of Jesus Christ I suffer the loss of all things in order to gain Christ."

Knowing Christ is not automatic. It is very true that the mind of the flesh can never know the things of God. The mind of the flesh will despise the things of God. Naturally speaking, in ourselves, in our flesh, it is all blind darkness against God. It is all rebellion and opposition towards God. It is true that unless God reveals His Son in us we do not know anything spiritually. Do not think by studying or by searching you can find God. You can know much about God, much about Christ, but you do not know Him in your very being. And because of this there is no transforming power. You may have a full knowledge of Jesus Christ, and yet you do not grow an inch spiritually. We need revelation, and thank God He is a God of revelation. It is His delight to reveal His Son in us. God wants to show us Christ all day long.

I often say whenever you go to see a family with a newborn baby, as you step into the door the first thing they will show you is their newborn son. That is their delight. And that is the way our God is. Not only has He revealed Christ Jesus to us as our Savior; it is His pleasure to reveal all of His Son to us. Revelation comes from God, and it is not difficult because it is a delight for Him to do that. But why is it that we do not receive revelation? There is standing within us something against that revelation and it is our old mind. It is our flesh. It is our old life within us, and these things are resisting the revelation of Jesus Christ to us. Whenever God reveals anything of His Son to us, immediately there rises up an opposition, a rejection, even hatred within us. And that is where spiritual travail comes in. In the past what we considered as precious, what we considered as our very life, when revelation of Jesus Christ came to us, there was a conflict of interest; there was a cross in our life. And what is our response? Do we exercise our spirit in the sense that we are willing to count all things as dross for the excellency of the knowledge of Jesus Christ?

To put it in another way, is our knowledge, our love, our clinging to things earthly preventing, opposing, hindering the revelation of Jesus Christ in our life? The problem does not come from God; the problem is in us. That problem needs to be solved, and it takes a lifetime to solve.

Our Lord Jesus said, "If anyone wants to come after Me, he has to deny himself, take up his cross daily, and follow Me." If we try to save our own lives, our self-life, we lose it. If for His sake we are willing to lose our self-life, we gain it to eternity. This is a spiritual law of spiritual growth. And today you find that God's people neglect it; not only neglect it, they even oppose it. We like to hear something that is pleasing to our natural ear, to our natural life. "Everything is all right. Go ahead. Do whatever you want, and you will end up in heaven." Wonderful! But that is dangerous. Without spiritual travail we are not able to gain Christ. The measure that we are willing to count all things as dross will be the measure of our spiritual growth in stature. So do not forget that.

How can we grow spiritually? Spiritual growth means only one thing. It means that the life of Christ in us grows into maturity. It is not our old life that grows into maturity.

That is the opposite. It is the life of Christ in us that grows into maturity. It should be a spiritually natural growth. But unfortunately, there is another life that becomes the enemy of that spiritual growth; therefore travail and suffering comes. But these sufferings are not in vain. These sufferings are with a purpose. Our flesh may suffer but the Christ-life in us will increase. And that is the only way to know Christ.

So I wonder why it is that God's people, after they are saved and after being a Christian for maybe ten, twenty, or thirty years, know a lot but grow very little? I have been asking this question for a long, long time. Why is it that God's people do not grow spiritually? Why do they not grow in the knowledge of Christ Jesus, knowing Christ deeper and deeper, seeing Christ as God the Father sees Him? That is spiritual growth. Why is there not much growth among God's people? Is it because we have a false idea of growth? Is it because we are lacking in travail? We really do not struggle before God? We really are not violent to ourselves? You remember the Bible says, "The kingdom of the heavens is to be gained by violence and the violent gain it." That does not mean violence to others; it means violence to our self, denying self. And if we do not deny our self, if we try to gratify our self, satisfy our self, give in to our self all the time, and even neglect the pleading of the Holy Spirit in our spirit, no wonder we do not grow. So spiritual growth, knowing Christ, requires, demands spiritual travail.

Are we daily travailing? Thank God the Holy Spirit is within us. We do not need to try to find things to deny. We do not even need to search our mind to see things we should repent of. That would be false. That would bring us into trouble. The Holy Spirit is within us. He is so wise. He knows our frame and He will bring to our remembrance. He will touch our conscience and speak to us in a still, small voice. He will shine His inner light upon our spirit, and we will begin to see that there is something that is standing in the way of our spiritual growth, and God demands that it be removed. Are we willing to deny our self, to lose our soul-life, as it were? We may suffer a little bit but that suffering is full of meaning because it brings us to Christ. That is gaining Christ. And this is a lifetime of pursuing. Even when the apostle Paul was in the Roman prison and he wrote the letter to the Philippians, he said, "I do not say that I have already possessed. I want to apprehend that for which I was apprehended. I am forgetting that which is behind and I am stretching myself towards the goal before me."

Travail for Sonship

The second area is travailing for sonship. God's purpose is not just to bring us into His family as babes. He wants us to grow into maturity, to be sons and daughters that can bear responsibility with our Lord Jesus. That is God's purpose, and for that purpose we have to travail.

Romans 8 makes it very clear. Even the whole universe is groaning. If we have spiritual ears we can hear the groaning of the trees, the groaning of the universe. They do not groan because of themselves; they are under corruption, emptiness, and vanity. It is because of man. It is man who brings the whole world into vanity, into corruption. So they are groaning for the day of freedom, but they cannot be freed until the manifestation of the sons of God, until God's children have grown up. And not only the whole universe, but the whole world is groaning around us. We who are the first fruits of the Holy Spirit are also groaning within ourselves. We want to grow.

I always remember when my youngest sister was just five or six years old. She had a cousin her age, and one day they were sitting on the stairway talking and somebody heard them. They were groaning. They said, "We are the littlest in the family. Our bigger sisters and brothers have so many privileges that we do not have." So they groaned because of their littleness.

Are you groaning within your spirit because you are still a babe? Or do you feel very comfortable being a babe in Christ? The life within us is a growing life, and because of that it is groaning within us. It is groaning for sonship, groaning for the day that we will be placed as sons, groaning for the day that we may be able to share not only our inheritance but also our responsibility with Christ Jesus, groaning for a day when we can reign with Christ. Do not think that reigning with Christ means that you are above everybody, giving orders and being served. The Lord said, "I am among you as one who serves instead of being served." Are we groaning for sonship? We groan because we realize that within us there is opposition. There is hindrance; there is that which leads us astray, and we do groan over it. You do not know how you can overcome it. You wrestle with it. You try to pray but you do not know how, and the Holy Spirit groans within you. God knows the mind of the Spirit, and somehow the whole thing begins to clear up. You begin to grow a little bit more.

Is that our experience? Why is it that God's people do not grow spiritually? It is because they are too comfortable with their present situation. They like to be babes in Christ and be taken care of by everybody. If anything is a little late they just cry and they are catered to. Do you want to be like that and make your Father sorrowful? We need to travail into sonship.

Travail for Souls

The third area is travailing for souls, just like the apostle Paul. In Romans 9 he said, "When I am thinking of my kinsmen, my brethren in the flesh, I have great grief. I am willing to be accursed from Christ and let my brethren be blessed." He travailed for his brethren, and he travailed for souls. I believe that as soon as you are saved there is a spiritual instinct within you. As Christ travailed for your soul, so when you are saved, automatically you feel within you a travail for the ones you love. If that kind of travail is absent I wonder whether you are saved. Have you ever travailed in prayer for any soul?

I remember brother Watchman Nee, after he was saved he tried to win his fellow students. He approached them, attacked them everywhere until his fellow students avoided him. One day he met Miss Groves, a fellow worker of Miss Barber. And Miss Groves asked him how many he had won to Christ.

He said, "None, but I preach Christ. It is their fault they did not believe."

So Miss Groves said, "Have you ever prayed for them?"

"Never!"

Miss Groves said, "You better pray for them because it is not you who saves them; it is Christ who saves them." So he put all these names in his book and prayed for them diligently, and within a short period one after another got saved.

Brothers and sisters, have you ever travailed for your father, for your mother, for your son, for your daughter, for your friend, for somebody? We need to travail for them.

Travail for the Church

The fourth area is travailing for the church. Paul travailed for the body of Christ. He travailed for the Corinthian church. He said, "I am willing to spend and be spent for you. Even if the more I love you, the less I am loved, I am willing to do that."

To the Ephesian church he said, "Day and night I preach and share with you the full counsel of God with tears."

To the Colossian church he said, "I travail to fill up that which is behind of the tribulation of Christ for the body's sake."

In other words, knowing that he is a member in the body of Christ he wants to see that body grow into maturity and he travails for it. Do we travail for the church? Do we travail because of all the divisions in the body of Christ? We need to travail to keep the spirit of the unity of the body of Christ. We need to pay a cost even for that reason. We need to travail in giving ourselves to minister to our brothers and sisters in a way that God has gifted us. It is not just being ministered to. We have our little part to play in the house of God, and in doing that we may be misunderstood. Sometimes we will be rejected. Thank God for that because it is through rejection or mistakes that we learn to submit ourselves under the headship of Christ so that the body may be increased with the increase of God. We find that we are to be involved in all these four areas.

HOW DO WE BEGIN TO TRAVAIL?

How do we begin? This spiritual travailing is not something we can work up ourselves. It is the love of God that constrains us. How we need to live close to God! How we need to meditate upon the love of Christ until we are so constrained that we will likewise have such love.

Do you love yourself? Everybody does. But you love the wrong self. You love the old self. You should love the new self. If you love the new self you will begin to travail for it. You will begin to pray for it. You will begin to be willing to pay any cost for it. Love is the beginning, and love is the force behind travail.

When the Lord gives you a burden within for yourself, for the sake of Christ, for other people, for the church, the best way and the highest way to express it is by prayer. Pray because this is something beyond us. If we can do anything without prayer it is a warning sign. Who is doing it? So we need to give ourselves to prayer and more prayer. Pray for all these things.

As we begin to pray we must give ourselves totally to God, willing to pay any cost. That is why before we build anything we need to sit down and count the cost. Are you willing to pay the cost? Unless you do that you may lay the foundation to build a tower but not complete it, and you will be a laughingstock. Count the cost, until by the grace of God, the mercy of God, you are willing to give yourself totally, completely to Him.

Begin small. Don't be so ambitious and try to pray great prayers, try to do many things. Begin small. That will deliver you from yourself. And in the measure of the Spirit of God working in you, you begin to grow. And if you are faithful in small things God will give you bigger things.

These are the practical ways of entering into this matter of spiritual travail. So may the Lord start it with each and every one of us. God bless you.

Chapter 3

QUESTIONS & ANSWERS

This is a question and answer time, and I want to explain what it means. If there are academic questions, man may be able to help, but if there are spiritual questions no man can help; no man can answer. But thank God, the answer is there, and I believe you all know it. It is Christ. So do not expect man to answer your spiritual questions; you have to go to the Lord for the answer. And you will find that if you try to get an answer from man it is very easy for you because you do not need to pay a cost. But if you try to get an answer from God, beware. There is a cost you have to pay.

We will use this opportunity to encourage one another, and as your fellow pilgrim all I can do is share and encourage. We are all learners. No man has ever graduated from the school of Christ. Brother Nee was advising a young medical doctor who was going to India as a missionary, and the brother asked him what he should do. Brother Nee said, "You need to hang a red sign with the letter *L* on it around your neck." In England when you are learning to drive, that is the sign you have to hang on your neck. So brother Nee said, "You go as a missionary, not to teach but to learn."

And dear brother and sisters, are we glad that we are all learners and we can encourage one another on the way upward?

Q: It was mentioned that one of the characteristics of spiritual travail is brokenness. Could you share some more light on this?

Q: What are the basic differences of a broken soul and an unbroken soul? Could an unbroken soul also enter into spiritual travail? Please provide some examples.

Q: Out of death comes life, but my experience tells me that although I consider myself having died several times, sometimes it pops up again. It seems that these are just fake deaths of self-life. How can we experience true death to our self-life so that the life of Christ might live out?

Q: In Philippians 3:10-11 it seems to me that the fellowship of His sufferings can only happen after we are standing on the ground of resurrection life. Could you shed some light on the relationship between the resurrection life and the spiritual travail? How can we always live on resurrection life?

Q: Could you clarify what the outcome of spiritual travail is? How can we put the outcome in the most simple and practical terms? Is the fruit or outcome of spiritual travail the manchild as mentioned in Revelation 12:5, or the bride of Christ in Revelation 19:7, or many sons in glory Romans 8:29?

BROKENNESS

First of all, what is brokenness? Brokenness refers to the breaking of the outward man. It is the soul-life that must be broken in order that the Christ-life in our spirit may be released. And we know in all spiritual experience it has to come from the spirit. It will touch the soul and the body but the origin has to begin in the spirit. It has to be a spiritual exercise, and spiritual travail no doubt is a spiritual exercise. Now in order for that which comes out of our spirit to be pure, our outward man, the soul-life has to be broken. Otherwise, whatever comes out will be a mixture; it will be impure. And God is a God of purity. Spiritual value actually rests in spiritual purity. So you can see right away that in this matter of spiritual travail brokenness is a must. But I am afraid among God's people the concept of brokenness is not quite accurate. Some people say that once you have experienced this brokenness then you are safe for life, that whatever comes afterwards must be of the spirit and not of the soul. Now that kind of concept is not accurate.

Spiritual things do not really begin with you. They always begin with God. God reveals, and under His revelation we know what needs to be broken. Otherwise, if you try to break yourself you will kill yourself. So revelation is actually the beginning of all spiritual experience. But when you think of revelation, probably your concept is inaccurate because you think of revelation as something tremendous, earth-shaking, and unless it is that kind there is no revelation. Not so!

Our dear brother Watchman Nee tells us that in our lifetime we may have one or two drastic revelations that seem to really change our life tremendously, but we should receive revelation day by day. Otherwise, how can we walk before God? As He reveals we follow.

So in this matter of brokenness it is the same thing. In our spiritual life there may come a day when there is such a drastic experience of brokenness it seems to revolutionize our life, but that does not mean because we have had such an experience therefore we are broken for life. Our self-life is very subtle. We probably have to be broken again and again. So brokenness is actually a progressive experience. For other people it is the opposite. They may be broken gradually, little by little, until one day there is a real brokenness.

Let me illustrate. What is the apostle Paul's experience? On the road to Damascus the light of God came upon him and he became a broken person. It changed him completely. But that does not mean he did not still have trials, he did not have to struggle, he did not have to be continually broken. You remember Romans 7. Some people say this may refer to Paul before he was converted, but I personally feel that it was after he had his mind renewed because it is a battle between the mind and the law in his body.

In the life of Jacob you find that God was trying to break him again and again. After he fled from his home, for twenty years God worked upon him to break him down but he was such a strong person. Then at Peniel, finally he wrestled with God, and God touched his thigh. He became a broken person. But even after he was broken there were still instances when the old sly Jacob came back up, and he could not have a good time. So brokenness is a spiritual principle. It is a basic principle for every believer who wants to grow spiritually; you have to experience it.

CAN AN UNBROKEN SOUL HAVE SPIRITUAL TRAVAIL?

Can an unbroken soul have spiritual travail? What do you think? Even before brokenness there can be some spiritual travail. Think of that! After you are saved do you ever pray and travail for the ones you love? Have you already experienced brokenness? No. It is true that in that kind of travail there is much that is worldly, self-centered, out of your own self. When you see other people perish, it may not touch you but when you think that your loved ones will perish, that worries you and you start to pray. There is some travailing but again it is very mixed. There may be a tiny little bit from the spirit but mostly it is from your soul-life. But as the Lord begins to purify you and you begin to pray not for your own sake but the sake of the Lord, you get it.

Take Hannah for instance. Hannah did not have a son. Can you imagine she never prayed for that son? Now if you are a woman I believe you will pray very earnestly to get a son. But God did not answer her until she came to a day when she realized that she wanted a son not for herself but for the Lord.

It is true, the purer our spirit is, the more broken our self-life is, the more effective will be our spiritual travail. But thank God, even after we are saved, that very life within us, the very Holy Spirit who indwells us, begins to work.

THE POWER OF HIS RESURRECTION

It is very true that the fellowship of Christ's suffering that Paul mentions in Philippians 3 follows the power of His resurrection. Any fellowship of His suffering, which includes spiritual travail, has to be the Lord working in our life. Otherwise, we cannot join with the Lord in His suffering. You have to see that it is not by your own life that you can travail spiritually. When you have spiritual travail, your soul-life suffers; that is true. But that does not mean that true spiritual travail comes from your soul. Your soul-life is affected because it is really the object of brokenness, but spiritual travail is carried on not by your soul-life; it is by your spirit-life. So you need to see what your spirit-life is. Your spirit-life is nothing but the life of Christ, and His life is the power of resurrection because He says, "I am the resurrection and the life." So I think it is very clear that spiritual travail is not of man; it is of God. It is the Spirit of God that moves upon your inner man, the Christ-life in you, and from that Christ-life there is a travail that begins from heaven to earth and then from earth back to heaven. And that is what prayer really is.

I believe even though we may not have reached a summit in our spiritual travail, and most likely we have not, yet I believe that more or less we have tasted something like it. And in order that this spiritual travail may really increase, which is not for ourselves but for the purpose of God, our outward man has to be broken. The problem is we do not realize how strong our soul-life is. In the measure of the breaking of the outward man will be the measure of the release of the inner man, which means we are more ready for spiritual travail.

In spiritual things it is never something that is merely an outward matter. It is always an inward experience. So the deeper you experience that breaking of your outward man, the more you will be prepared for spiritual travail.

THE FRUIT OF SPIRITUAL TRAVAIL

What will be the fruit of it? In reading the Scriptures you will find that through spiritual travail, through your passion for Christ and nothing but Christ, it will gradually fulfill God's purpose concerning His Son, that His Son may be all and in all in your life, and He may sum up all things in your life. At the same time you will be transformed and conformed to the image of Christ. You will be used of God as Paul was used to help, to bring people to the Lord and to help perfect them in Christ. And by doing that, the church, the body of Christ will be built.

Thank God, our Lord Jesus travails for the church. He brings it to birth, and He is continuing to travail for His church. And by the grace of God we are to share in that which is lacking of the tribulation of Christ for His body. This is not in a redeeming, atoning sense, but in the sense of encouraging, helping, ministering, uniting brothers and sisters in order that we may grow together to be a full grown body, full of the stature of Christ for the coming of the Bridegroom. So as you read the Scriptures you can say that the fruit may be the manchild in Revelation 12, it may be the bride in Revelation 19, and without doubt it is the eternal bride in Revelation 21 and 22. Thank God, He who has purposed it has perfected it.

www.ingramcontent.com/pod-product-compliance
Lightning Source LLC
Chambersburg PA
CBHW060637030426
42337CB00018B/3394